Original title:
Steps to the Divine Presence

Copyright © 2024 Book Fairy Publishing
All rights reserved.

Author: Elias Seraphim
ISBN HARDBACK: 978-9916-87-853-8
ISBN PAPERBACK: 978-9916-87-854-5

## Pathways of the Sacred Heart

In gardens lush, the spirit grows,
Where every prayer like water flows.
Embraced by grace, we walk the way,
The sacred path, where love holds sway.

Each step we take, a whisper sweet,
In unity, our souls shall meet.
Through trials faced, we find our tune,
Our hearts alight beneath the moon.

## Ascendancy of the Spirit

Beneath the arch of heaven's dome,
We rise with faith, in flesh and bone.
The spirit's call, a gentle breeze,
Awakens us, our hearts at ease.

As mountains high, our hopes ascend,
In grace, we find our journey's end.
Together bound in joy and light,
We chase the stars throughout the night.

## Climbing the Celestial Staircase

Step by step, we strive and climb,
In faith, we conquer space and time.
With every prayer, we lift our eyes,
To reach the realms where grace complies.

The staircase shines with love's embrace,
A heavenly path, a sacred place.
As angels hum a chorus bright,
We find our peace in endless light.

## **Journey Toward the Holy Light**

With humble hearts, we start the quest,
To seek the light, our souls expressed.
Through valleys deep and mountains grand,
We follow faith, and hand in hand.

Each trial faced brings wisdom sweet,
In every struggle, love's heartbeat.
Together we will find the way,
Toward holy light, a bright new day.

## The Path Beneath the Wings

In whispers soft, the angels glide,
Guiding souls with arms open wide.
Their feathers sweep the weary ground,
In sacred light, lost dreams are found.

Through valleys deep, where shadows weep,
Faith takes root, promises to keep.
Each step forward, a prayer released,
In the embrace of wings, doubts cease.

## The Luminescence of Faith

Stars align in a celestial dance,
Illuminated by a holy chance.
Hearts ablaze with love divine,
In faith's embrace, our souls entwine.

Small flickers grow to radiant light,
Casting away the cloak of night.
In every prayer, a beacon shines,
Guiding us through life's winding lines.

## **Pathways to the Sacred Light**

Through rugged roads we seek the dawn,
With every step, our fears are gone.
Faith like a lantern, steady and bright,
Leading us onward in the night.

Mountains high and rivers wide,
In trust we walk, and never slide.
Each pathway carved by love's own hand,
Bringing us closer to the promised land.

## **Journey into the Holy Embrace**

We wander forth with hearts sincere,
In every smile, the Lord is near.
With open arms, He draws us close,
In sacred silence, we find our repose.

Through trials faced, our spirits soar,
In unity, we seek much more.
Together bound in love's great grace,
We find our home in the holy embrace.

## The Labyrinth of Spiritual Awakening

In shadows deep, the heart does roam,
Seeking light, it finds a home.
Through winding paths and whispered grace,
Awakening soul, embrace the space.

The mirror gleams with truth so bright,
Each turn reveals the sacred light.
In every step, the spirit sings,
A dance of joy, the freedom brings.

## The Sacred River of Yearning

Flowing gently, love's soft stream,
Carrying hearts on a vibrant dream.
In its depths, the soul finds peace,
A fountain of hope that will never cease.

Rippling waters, secrets shared,
Across the banks, souls bared.
With every wave, a prayer ascends,
The river's song, where being blends.

## Divine Threads in the Fabric of Life


Woven tightly, patterns gleam,
In every stitch, the heart's own dream.
Threads of mercy, hope, and strife,
In sacred tapestry, the dance of life.

Each knot a promise, love's embrace,
In unity found, we find our place.
The loom of fate, a crafting hand,
In service to the greater plan.

## Illuminated Paths of Prayer

Beneath the stars, the pilgrims tread,
With whispered wishes softly said.
In the glow of faith, they rise and kneel,
Their yearnings woven into the steel.

Each footfall lights the way ahead,
In grace's hue, all fears are shed.
Together joined in sacred breath,
Life's journey cast beyond the death.

## Beneath the Veil of the Infinite

In silence, shadows gently dance,
The spirit whispers, finds its chance.
A tapestry of stars unwinds,
Each heartbeat echoes, love it binds.

Beneath the veil, we seek the light,
The sacred truth, a holy sight.
With every breath, we kneel in grace,
In the vastness of this sacred space.

The beauty lies within the still,
In humble hearts, we find His will.
A gentle touch, a guiding hand,
In the embrace of the Divine, we stand.

## Echoes of the Sacred Heart

Listen closely, the heart does sing,
A melody of peace, it brings.
In the rhythm of love divine,
All souls together, forever entwined.

Through tribulation, faith shines bright,
A beacon glowing in the night.
With every echo, we draw near,
In sacred gathering, void of fear.

The warmth of grace, a tender balm,
In trials faced, we find the calm.
With hearts ablaze, in unity,
We soar on wings of purity.

## The Illumined Pathway of Surrender

Upon the path, we tread with care,
In gentle whispers, truth we share.
Surrender softens every ache,
In yielding, we discern the wake.

Each step we take, the light unfolds,
In heart and mind, the story told.
The burdens lift, the spirit flies,
In surrender's grace, our soul complies.

Trusting the journey, we embrace,
The wisdom found in silent space.
With open hearts, we humbly climb,
In love's embrace, we spend our time.

## Songs of the Seraphim

High above, the seraphim soar,
Their songs resound forevermore.
In celestial harmonies they sing,
A chorus loud that heavens bring.

With wings of light, they grace the skies,
In every note, a prayer complies.
For every heart in quest of peace,
Their melodies bring sweet release.

Together, all the faithful rise,
In love's pure light, we see the skies.
With every song, our spirits lift,
In sacred echoes, love is the gift.

## The Silent Heartbeat of Existence

In the stillness, whispers weave,
Threads of fate that we perceive.
Nature cradles every sigh,
In its arms, our spirits fly.

Through the shadows, light does bloom,
Guiding souls amidst the gloom.
Every heartbeat sings a song,
Echoing where we belong.

In the quiet, wisdom flows,
Ancient truths that time bestows.
Every moment, sacred grace,
In the silence, find our place.

Life unfolds like petals soft,
In the heart, a yearning oft.
Silent paths, the journey's art,
In existence, love imparts.

## In Pursuit of the Infinite Embrace

Boundless skies where dreams take flight,
Seeking warmth in cosmic light.
Every star a guiding flame,
In the darkness, call His name.

Waves of grace, they wash the shore,
Beyond the self, we seek for more.
Hearts entwined in love's embrace,
In His arms, we find our place.

Wandering through this vast expanse,
In the dance, we take a chance.
Every breath a prayer we share,
In pursuit, in love, laid bare.

Fingers trace the woven fate,
In the stillness, we create.
With each heartbeat, love ignites,
In the night, our souls take flight.

## Song of the Wandering Soul

In the twilight, shadows roam,
Yearning for a distant home.
Footsteps echo through the night,
Guided by the inner light.

Every sorrow blends with peace,
In the struggle, hearts release.
Wandering through valleys wide,
Trusting in the path we bide.

Songs of ancients fill the air,
Melodies of love and care.
Singing softly to the stars,
Hearts united, near or far.

Through the trials, hope will soar,
Finding strength on heaven's shore.
Every soul a story tells,
In the silence, love compels.

## Ascending the Hall of Mirrors

In this hall where shadows gleam,
Reflection bends the truth, a dream.
Every glance reveals the past,
In the present, shadows cast.

Mirrors whisper, truths untold,
In their depths, our hearts behold.
Every face, a different guise,
In the stillness, wisdom lies.

Climbing higher, truths align,
In the light, our souls divine.
Every glance, a fleeting spark,
Illuminating paths gone dark.

With each step, we cast away,
Fears that hold our spirits sway.
In the mirrors, love's embrace,
Guiding us to our true place.

## The Heart's Pathway to Enlightenment

In silence I seek the truth divine,
Wandering paths where shadows align.
A whispering breeze guides my way,
To the light of a dawning day.

With every step, I shed my fears,
Offering prayers through joyful tears.
In the garden of spirit, I plant my soul,
Harvesting wisdom that makes me whole.

Each heartbeat a rhythm, a sacred song,
Echoing love where I belong.
The journey unfolds with each breath I take,
Marking the steps that faith will make.

As the sun sets on the world's face,
I gather the stars in a cosmic embrace.
For in darkness, the light shall bloom,
Illuminating the heart's eternal room.

## Wings of Serendipitous Grace

Through valleys of doubt, my spirit soars,
On wings of grace, I open new doors.
Embracing the gifts that life doth impart,
The whispers of hope fill my grateful heart.

In moments of silence, I hear the call,
Guided by love that transcends it all.
With faith as my anchor, I rise and glide,
Trusting the journey, the universe wide.

Every serendipity, a lesson bestowed,
Light on the path where the sacred flowed.
In union with all, I find my place,
Forever uplifted by serendipitous grace.

With each gentle breeze, I am reborn,
From shadows of night to the blush of dawn.
Embracing the mystery, I'm led by the light,
As wings of grace guide me through the night.

## The Hearth of Inner Sanctuary

In silence deep, I seek the light,
A sacred space within my heart.
The warmth of faith, a guiding spark,
It whispers peace, never to part.

With prayers entwined, my spirit soars,
Through trials faced, in love I stand.
Each breath a hymn, each sigh a song,
In this refuge, I feel the hand.

The candle's glow, my only guide,
Illuminates the path I tread.
In trust, I leave my fears behind,
Held close by grace, where I am led.

Here in this hearth, my soul finds rest,
A holy place where dreams take flight.
In stillness, hope begins to bloom,
In this sanctuary, pure and right.

## In the Shadow of the Holy

Beneath the arch of sacred skies,
I wander lightly, heart in roam.
In whispered winds, the Spirit speaks,
Renewing faith, I find my home.

Among the trees, I hear the song,
Of angels guiding, ever near.
Their shadows cast upon my path,
In stillness, all my doubts disappear.

The sacred voice that calls my name,
Echoes softly in the night.
In shadows' grace, I feel the peace,
With every breath, the world feels right.

In the embrace of holy light,
I walk the line of earth and grace.
In reverence, I lift my soul,
To find my truth in love's embrace.

## Feet on Earth, Eyes on Heaven

With feet on earth, I stand so firm,
In steadfast grace, my heart believes.
I gaze above, where dreams arise,
In faith, I seek what love achieves.

The clouds may part to let love shine,
A promise whispered in the night.
In every trial, I'll find my way,
Like stars that glimmer, bold and bright.

The beauty here, a sacred thread,
Connected deeply, gold and pure.
With every step, I walk in trust,
United in the heart's rapport.

From earth to sky, my spirit flies,
Each moment filled with hope and prayer.
In harmony, we dance as one,
A tapestry of love laid bare.

## Embracing the Radiant Known

The dawn unfolds with gentle grace,
Awakening the morning light.
In every heart, a spark ignites,
A promise of the day so bright.

In every glance, the love unfolds,
Through kindness shared, we find our way.
The radiant souls, in unity,
Embrace the blessings of today.

With open arms, we gather near,
In laughter's song and sweet refrain.
The world transformed in love's gentle glow,
In gratitude, we welcome rain.

Together bound by faith and hope,
We rise as one, as seasons flow.
With courage deep, we'll walk this path,
Embracing all the radiant known.

# A Covenant with the Celestial

In whispers soft, the heavens speak,
A promise held, both pure and meek.
The stars align to guide our way,
In faith we walk, come what may.

With every breath, a sacred trust,
In light we dwell, in love we must.
The spirit sings, a song divine,
A bond unbroken, forever thine.

Through trials faced, we find our grace,
As shadows fall, the light we chase.
In unity, our hearts entwined,
A covenant, through space and time.

Together we rise, in harmony,
Guided by the unseen mystery.
With every step, we seek the truth,
In love's embrace, reclaim our youth.

## Radiance of the Unseen

In the stillness, a whisper calls,
Echoes of light through shadowed halls.
The unseen hand, it softly guides,
In every heart, a truth abides.

The sun may hide, but hope remains,
In quiet moments, joy sustains.
A radiance bright shines from within,
Illuminating where we've been.

With every prayer, the spirit soars,
As love ignites, opening doors.
In sacred trust, we find our way,
The unseen path, our hearts obey.

When twilight falls, we stand as one,
In gratitude for lessons won.
The radiance flows, a sacred stream,
Uniting all in one great dream.

## Lifting Eyes to the Horizon

With eyes uplifted, we gaze afar,
Chasing the light from each bright star.
The horizon whispers promises new,
A journey blessed, we embark true.

Each dawn brings hope, a rising sun,
In every heart, new battles won.
Hands joined in prayer, we seek the light,
Guided by faith, dispelling night.

In steps of courage, our spirits soar,
Embracing grace forevermore.
The horizon calls, a beckoning light,
With love as our guide, we take flight.

Through valleys deep and mountains high,
Our spirits dance beneath the sky.
With every breath, we find our way,
Lifting our souls to a brand new day.

## The Holy Quest of the Soul

In every heartbeat, a quest unfolds,
A journey ancient, a tale retold.
Through trials faced, the soul will grow,
In searching depths, the light will show.

With every tear, a lesson learned,
In love's embrace, our hearts are turned.
The quest divine, a sacred call,
To rise above, to never fall.

Each step we take, with grace in tow,
Through valleys low and peaks aglow.
In fervent prayer, we find our way,
The holy path, we walk each day.

With faith as armor, we stand strong,
In unity, we sing our song.
The holy quest, our souls entwined,
In love and light, true peace we find.

# A Quest for Celestial Truth

In silent prayers, we seek the light,
Awakening hearts in the still of night.
Whispers of wisdom guide our way,
To realms where shadows cannot stay.

With faith as our compass, we ascend,
To explore the paths where divinity blends.
Each step a promise, each breath a grace,
In the boundless love of a sacred space.

The stars above sing songs of old,
Of secrets kept and stories told.
In the tapestry of time, we weave,
The truths that nourish, and those that leave.

Oh questing soul, be not afraid,
For in every heart, heaven's laid.
In the search for truth, we find our home,
A journey together, never alone.

## Mosaics of Mystical Awareness

In the garden of thoughts, colors bloom,
Fragments of dreams dispel the gloom.
Each moment a piece, each glance a door,
Unfolding the mysteries we long to explore.

Within the whispers of the ancient trees,
Lies the wisdom that flows like the breeze.
Mosaics crafted from joy and pain,
Reveal the beauty in love's refrain.

With open hearts, we gather the light,
Illuminating paths through the darkest night.
In unity, the visions combine,
Creating a tapestry divine.

Through each moment, awareness grows,
Connecting the dots where the spirit flows.
In sacred stillness, we come to see,
The interconnectedness of you and me.

## **The Bridge to Sacred Understanding**

In quietude, the spirit speaks,
Through valleys low and mountain peaks.
Building bridges with every prayer,
Connecting hearts, uniting care.

Across the waters of doubt and fear,
We walk the path, the truth draws near.
Each step a promise, each word we share,
Strengthens the bond of love and prayer.

With grace we journey, hand in hand,
Opening minds to a sacred land.
In understanding, we find our peace,
In love's embrace, all strife shall cease.

Together we rise, forever strong,
In the symphony of the sacred song.
With faith as our guide, we cross the span,
A bridge to understanding, woman and man.

## The Radiance of Our Seeking

In the depths of silence, a glow appears,
The radiance born from love's own tears.
Each moment of seeking, a spark ignites,
Guiding our souls through the endless nights.

With open eyes, we glimpse the divine,
In every heartbeat, the universe shines.
Awakening spirits, we rise and soar,
In the light of seeking, we yearn for more.

The journey unfolds like a sacred dance,
Each step in rhythm, each breath a chance.
In the light of truth, we discover our way,
Illuminating paths of hope each day.

As seekers of wisdom, we stand as one,
Embracing the light, the moon, and the sun.
In the radiance of our seeking, we find,
The warmth of connection, spirit intertwined.

## Ascend to the Celestial Realm

In quiet prayer, we raise our eyes,
To the heavens where our spirit flies.
With faith as wings, we seek the light,
In divine embrace, we find our might.

The stars above, a guiding stone,
Whispering truths we've always known.
To walk in grace, our hearts aligned,
In love's pure glow, our souls unwind.

Through trials faced, we find our way,
In moments still, we choose to pray.
Each step adorned with hope anew,
In every breath, Thy will be true.

So let us soar on sacred winds,
With every heartbeat, faith rescinds.
The path before, it's clear to see,
Ascend we will, eternally.

## **Footprints on the Sacred Journey**

Each step we take, a story told,
In sacred earth, where dreams unfold.
With every footprint left behind,
A trail of love for all mankind.

Through valleys deep and mountains high,
We walk with faith, our spirits nigh.
In trials faced, together stand,
Guided by His gracious hand.

The journey long, with lessons learned,
In each setback, our hearts have turned.
A bond of souls, in light we grow,
As footprints mark our path below.

So let us tread with humble grace,
In every challenge, embrace His face.
In unity, we find our call,
Footprints in love, to heal us all.

## Climbing the Mountain of Grace

With each ascent, the peaks arise,
In holy stillness, beneath the skies.
We climb with courage, hearts alight,
Each step a prayer, a guiding light.

The mountain calls, a wisdom vast,
In sacred whispers, our fears surpassed.
Through trials steep, we rise anew,
In every struggle, His grace shines through.

The summit beckons, a promise sweet,
With faith as strength, we will not retreat.
In every heartbeat, a sacred trust,
We climb in love, united, we must.

Atop the heights, we breathe the air,
In pure connection, we find our prayer.
To climb the mountain, bright and wide,
In grace we dwell, our hearts abide.

## **Trails of the Transcendental**

Along the paths, where shadows play,
We seek the light of a brand new day.
In every footfall, a breath divine,
Through trials faced, forever shine.

With open hearts, we wander free,
In the sacred flow, we come to see.
The trails we tread, in unity,
Are echoes of eternal harmony.

As nature whispers, we find our peace,
In every heartbeat, our worries cease.
The journey holds a map of grace,
In every corner, we see His face.

So let us walk with mindful care,
Within each moment, find Him there.
On trails of love, we journey on,
In transcendental light, we're never gone.

## Embrace of the Radiant Light


In the dawn's embrace, rays unfold,
Whispers of warmth, both gentle and bold.
Heavenly grace spills from above,
A tapestry woven with threads of love.

Beneath the skies, our spirits ascend,
Vessels of faith, on Him we depend.
In every shadow, He shines so bright,
Guiding our hearts, the Radiant Light.

With open arms, we gather near,
Hearts intertwined, casting out fear.
In every heartbeat, His presence we feel,
In the embrace of His love, we heal.

Let the righteous dance, let praises soar,
In the shelter of grace, forevermore.
In the embrace of His wondrous might,
We find our strength in the Radiant Light.

## Lingering in the Presence

In quiet moments, we seek His face,
Lingering softly in sacred space.
Where silence speaks, and hearts unite,
Wrapped in the warmth of His holy light.

Time dances slow, as we breathe deep,
In His presence, our souls He keeps.
Melodies whispered in the still of night,
Drawing us closer, to that holy site.

Each prayer a note, in a symphony pure,
In His presence, our spirits endure.
With every heartbeat, His love resounds,
In the sacred silence, His grace abounds.

Here we find peace, in truth we stand,
Lingering softly, hand in hand.
In the echo of faith, we take flight,
Dancing forever in His light.

## The Invitation of Silence

In the hush of dawn, a call so clear,
The invitation of silence draws us near.
Where the weary find rest, and burdens cease,
In moments of stillness, we uncover peace.

Listen closely, the whispers unfold,
Secrets of the ages, in heartbeats told.
A sanctuary found, in quiet realms,
The spirit awakens, within us it swells.

Each breath a prayer, each sigh a song,
In the invitation, we all belong.
With minds unclouded, and souls so bright,
We soar through the darkness, into the light.

So linger a while, in this sacred space,
Embrace the silence, and taste His grace.
In the invitation, let your heart take flight,
Awakening joy in the quiet of night.

## Songs of the Seraphim

In heavenly courts, the seraphim sing,
Voices of worship, their praises they bring.
Around the throne, they circle and sway,
In harmony's grace, their spirits play.

With wings unfurled, like whispers of light,
They dance through the heavens, a glorious sight.
Each note a blessing, each melody true,
Songs of the seraphim, calling to you.

In the stillness, their echoes remain,
Filling our hearts with sacred refrain.
In the depths of our souls, their music unfolds,
A testament of love, in stories retold.

Let us join in, with hearts set free,
Singing along, in sweet harmony.
In the songs of the seraphim bright,
We find our place, in the arms of the Light.

## **In the Footsteps of the Beloved**

In quiet paths where shadows play,
We walk beside the blessed way.
Each step a prayer, each breath a song,
In love's embrace, where souls belong.

The whispers of the ancient trees,
Guide us gently with sacred ease.
In every moment, His light we seek,
In tender silence, our spirits speak.

Through valleys low and mountains high,
We carry hope, we do not sigh.
With every heartbeat, grace unfolds,
In humble hearts, His story holds.

To serve and love, our noble quest,
In the footsteps of the blessed.
With faith as lantern, we brightly shine,
In the circle of the divine.

## A Dance with the Divine

In the stillness of the twilight hour,
We feel the rush of sacred power.
A dance begins beneath the stars,
Where love transcends our earthly bars.

With every step, the world dissolves,
As we become, in joy, involved.
The heartbeat syncs with heaven's grace,
In every twirl, we seek His face.

The music swells, our spirits rise,
In the rhythm, a holy guise.
As souls entwined, we spin and sweep,
In the embrace, our secrets keep.

In union's light, we find our way,
A dance with the divine each day.
In love's cathedral, hearts aligned,
We weave a tapestry, divine.

## When Hearts Become Altar Flames

In whispered prayers, our spirits lift,
When hearts become the altar's gift.
A sacrifice of love and trust,
In burning flames, we rise from dust.

With every tear, a story told,
In ashes, hope and joy unfold.
The warmth of faith ignites the night,
As hearts ablaze, we seek the light.

In unity, our voices soar,
Each burning ember, wanting more.
Together, we transcend all fears,
When hearts become the altar's tears.

Through trials faced and dreams ignited,
In sacred fires, we're united.
With passion pure and souls aflame,
We worship in the beloved's name.

## Veils of Reverence Unfurled

In quiet rooms of whispered prayer,
Veils of reverence fill the air.
Each fold a story, softly spun,
In the tapestry, we are one.

As candles flicker, shadows dance,
In sacred stillness, hearts find chance.
The mysteries wrapped in gentle light,
Guide us softly towards the night.

With open hands and humble hearts,
We seek the source from which love starts.
In every crease, a grace revealed,
Veils of reverence gently healed.

With each exhale, we breathe Him in,
In the longing, our spirits spin.
As veils unfurl, the truth we find,
In sacred love, forever bind.

## The Gardens of Divine Longing

In quiet grace the gardens bloom,
With petals soft, dispelling gloom.
Each fragrant breath, a whispered prayer,
Inviting souls to linger there.

Beneath the arch of heaven's light,
The heart finds peace, the spirit's flight.
In every leaf, a sacred song,
A symphony where we belong.

Through paths of gold, and silver streams,
We walk in faith, fulfilling dreams.
With every step, divine embrace,
In seeking truth, we find our place.

Oh gardens vast, a holy shore,
Where love and light forever pour.
In every shade, a promise made,
In divine longing, we are swayed.

## A Tapestry of Faith's Journey

Threads of hope in colors bright,
Woven through the endless night.
Each stitch a story, rich and deep,
In faith's embrace, our souls we keep.

Patterns formed from trials shared,
In moments frail, our hearts are bared.
With every tear and joyful laugh,
Our lives entwined, a perfect craft.

The loom of time unravels fast,
Yet in this tapestry, we cast.
The dreams of many, strong and true,
We weave with love, our spirits new.

From simple strands, a vision grand,
In every knot, the guiding hand.
Together bound, in faith we rise,
A tapestry beneath the skies.

## The Circle of Eternal Wisdom

In circles wide, the wisdom flows,
A well of truth, where silence grows.
In stillness found, the answers dwell,
In every heart, a sacred well.

The ages turn, and time reveals,
The gentle touch that love conceals.
In every glance, a lesson learned,
In every heart, a flame that burned.

Around the wheel, our journeys spin,
In unity, the ties begin.
With open hearts, we seek the light,
In circles of the day and night.

Eternal truth, forever shared,
In every soul, divinely paired.
The circle holds, the wisdom shines,
In love and light, our spirit twines.

## **Divine Footfalls on Earthly Soil**

In softest steps, a presence wise,
Through earthly paths where beauty lies.
With every tread, the ground aglow,
A gentle warmth, a holy flow.

The whispers touch the silent air,
In fleeting moments, hearts laid bare.
With grace, the shadows fade away,
Revealing light in midst of grey.

Each footprint stamps a tale of grace,
In every soul, a warm embrace.
As we walk on this sacred ground,
In every heartbeat, love is found.

Divine the journey, each step true,
In earthly soil, our spirits grew.
With every footfall, hope ignites,
In divine love, the world unites.

## The Sanctuary of Inner Stillness

In quiet depths of ancient prayer,
Where whispers reign and burdens bare.
The heart finds peace in sacred grace,
In stillness, we behold His face.

Beneath the glow of candlelight,
We seek the truth in gentle night.
Each moment breathed, a sacred song,
A tranquil spirit, pure and strong.

The clouds part ways, the heavens sigh,
In solitude, the soul can fly.
The world's demands begin to cease,
Here in our hearts, we find our peace.

## Hallowed Ground Beneath Our Feet

On this earth, where shadows rest,
We tread on soil, divinely blessed.
Each step we take, a prayer in time,
In unity, our souls will climb.

The grass sings soft, the trees converse,
In nature's arms, we find our verse.
With every breath, the earth reveals,
Hallowed ground, where the spirit heals.

The mountains rise, the rivers flow,
In their embrace, our spirits grow.
Awake to wonder, we shall glean,
The sacred dance of all unseen.

## Radiant Reflections of the Soul

In mirrors deep, where silence glows,
The light within each being shows.
Our hearts, a canvas, love bestowed,
Radiant paths where wisdom flowed.

With every tear, a story shared,
In joy and sorrow, hearts are bared.
The colors blend, a vibrant hue,
Reflections of the pure and true.

We rise in grace, the spirit calls,
The radiant light within us sprawls.
Each journey taken, each step bold,
Embracing love, our tale unfolds.

## The Call of Holiness Beckons

O gentle whisper, soft and clear,
The call to holiness draws near.
In every heart, a sacred quest,
To walk in love, to truly rest.

The morning sun, a promise bright,
Awakens souls with golden light.
In every choice, a chance to grow,
The call of holiness we know.

With faith, we rise, unshakeable,
In unity, invincible.
The path ahead, though winding still,
The call of holiness, our will.

## Walking the Sacred Spiral

In the stillness of dawn, I tread,
Through whispers of light, by angels led.
Each step a prayer, each breath a song,
In the sacred spiral, where I belong.

Nature's embrace, the earth my guide,
In the circle of life, I shall abide.
The heavens above, the roots below,
In this dance of spirit, my heart shall glow.

With the pulse of the world beneath my feet,
In every heartbeat, the Divine I meet.
Moonlit shadows, the stars align,
In the sacred spiral, my soul entwines.

With every turn, I uncover grace,
In the vast expanse of this holy space.
Walking in faith, I feel the flow,
On this sacred journey, my spirit grows.

## A Pilgrim's Prayer Under Starlit Skies

Beneath the canopy of twinkling lights,
I seek Your presence on this sacred night.
With hands uplifted and heart sincere,
I offer this prayer, my soul draws near.

Guide my steps, O Light Divine,
Through valleys deep and mountain climb.
In shadows deep, Your love remains,
A truth unwavering, through joy and pain.

As stars bear witness to my quest,
With every heartbeat, I seek to rest.
In valleys of silence, Your whispers flow,
A pilgrim's prayer, in faith I sow.

Shower Your blessings, as night unfolds,
In starlit skies, Your story told.
With every breath, my spirit sings,
In this sacred moment, forgiveness brings.

## The Altar of the Seeking Heart

On the altar of my seeking heart,
I lay my dreams, each precious part.
With trust and hope, I light my way,
In reverence deep, I humbly pray.

What is found in silence rare,
Echoes of love fill the air.
In search of truth, I find my soul,
In the altar of faith, I am made whole.

Every question, a sacred spark,
A journey into the endless dark.
With every tear, I grow and learn,
In the sacred fire, my heart does burn.

O Divine Spirit, hear my plea,
In the mosaic of life, make me see.
The altar of love within me beats,
In every moment, Your grace repeats.

## The Veil Between Flesh and Spirit

In twilight's glow, the veil grows thin,
Between the seen and the unseen kin.
With gentle whispers, the spirit calls,
To transcend the flesh, where the heart enthralls.

In the sacred hush, I hear the sound,
Of timeless echoes, in silence profound.
Flesh may falter, yet spirit soars,
In this divine dance, my soul restores.

With each heartbeat, the veil does sway,
Leading my spirit to brighter day.
In the sacred embrace of love's light,
I navigate darkness, towards the bright.

Bridge the realms, O Holy One,
In the dance of existence, we're never done.
The veil between worlds ever so slight,
Guides me from shadow toward the light.

## Hints of the Holy in Everyday Life

In the morning light, a gentle breeze,
Whispers of grace among the trees.
Every smile shared, a sacred art,
Echoes of love that fill the heart.

In the soft rain that kisses the ground,
Life awakens, beauty is found.
A child's laughter, pure and bright,
Reveals the joy of heavenly light.

In the stillness of night, stars align,
Constellations of hope, a design.
Each moment fleeting, yet a sign,
Reminders of purpose, divine.

Every breath taken, a gift bestowed,
Paths of the faithful, where love flowed.
In simple acts, the holy glows,
Hints of the sacred, love bestows.

## Symphony of the Spirit's Ascent

In the quiet dusk, the heart takes flight,
Melodies rise to embrace the night.
Notes of devotion dance in the air,
A symphony woven with gentle care.

Voices uplifted, a chorus of praise,
Echoing prayers in a holy haze.
Each heartbeat a rhythm, a soulful refrain,
Guiding the spirit through joy and pain.

Wind through the trees, a whispering sound,
Nature's resonance, the sacred found.
With every heartbeat, a sacred quest,
In harmony's arms, the soul finds rest.

In the still of the night, a silence profound,
The spirit ascends, unbounded, unbound.
With faith as the melody, hope as the song,
Together we rise, where we all belong.

## Threads of Connection to the Divine

In each sacred thread, a story we weave,
Binding the moments we choose to believe.
Through trials and triumphs, entwined we stand,
Connected by grace, in the Father's hand.

In the warmth of a smile, a touch so kind,
Heaven's reflection in hearts intertwined.
Every shared tear, a testament true,
Threads of compassion, stitched anew.

In the gaze of a stranger, a spark is found,
Reminders of love that knows no bounds.
With voices united, we sing as one,
A tapestry rich, 'neath the same sun.

With each guiding hand, a path is laid,
Creating connections where grace is displayed.
In the fabric of life, we find our way,
Threads of the sacred, in bright array.

## Moments of Divine Interruption

In the hustle and rush of the daily grind,
A moment arrives, with peace intertwined.
A sudden stillness, a pause in the day,
When heaven's whispers gently sway.

A stranger's kindness, a hand outstretched,
In fleeting seconds, our hearts are fetched.
A laugh shared between souls, unexpected grace,
In divine interruption, we find our place.

Through trials that toy with the weary heart,
A glimpse of the holy, a precious part.
In shadows that linger, light breaks through,
In moments divine, the spirit renews.

As life unfolds, in mundane ways,
We glimpse the divine through the ordinary days.
In every heartbeat, in joy and strife,
Moments divine, the essence of life.

## Mapping the Sacred Topography

In the silence of the dawn, we seek,
Paths that lead to the divine peak.
Each step etched in sacred ground,
Whispers of truth in silence found.

Mountains rise like prayers on high,
Clouds embrace the searching sky.
Rivers flow with wisdom's grace,
Carving valleys in the holy space.

Let us wander through this land,
Guided by a gentle hand.
Stars above, the night's embrace,
Illumines every sacred place.

Every stone an ancient tale,
In the heart where spirits sail.
Mapping realms of spirit's lore,
Together, we shall seek and soar.

## Under the Gaze of the Eternal

Beneath the watchful cosmic eye,
We walk on earth, our souls a sigh.
Eternal light breaks through the shade,
In every moment, blessings laid.

Time flows softly, like a stream,
Each heartbeat a recurring dream.
In the stillness, we hear the call,
To rise, to love, to give our all.

Under skies of azure grace,
In the silence, we find our place.
Eternity breathes in our veins,
Binding joy with all its pains.

With hands uplifted, hearts unchained,
We gather strength from love unfeigned.
Under the gaze, we find our song,
Together in the light, we belong.

## **Meld in the Mystery of Being**

In the depths of night, we ponder,
Life's great questions, hearts grow fonder.
Mysteries weave like threads of gold,
In every story, truth unfolds.

Stars above, they shimmer bright,
Each a beacon in the night.
To meld our souls with all that is,
In quiet moments, we find bliss.

The cosmic dance, a sacred tie,
Binding earth and zephyr sky.
In the whispers of the breeze,
Find the essence, hearts at ease.

In the mystery, we shall dwell,
In the silence, all is well.
Being's joy, a sweet refrain,
In love's embrace, we break the chain.

## Gathering the Fragments of Light

In the shards of day that gleam,
We gather pieces, stitch a dream.
Fragments scattered, lost from sight,
Yet united in the purest light.

Each smile shared, a flickering flame,
In the darkness, call out a name.
Light within, we seek to find,
Healing whispers, hearts entwined.

With open arms, we bring them near,
Every joy, every silent tear.
Together, in the sacred space,
We weave a tapestry of grace.

As dawn breaks, we rise anew,
Mending hearts with love so true.
Gathering light from every source,
Together, we shall chart our course.

## Reflections on the Water of Grace

In silence, ripples dance with light,
Whispers of love in sacred flight.
Reflections deep in waters calm,
A glimpse of peace, a gentle balm.

Beneath the surface, truth resides,
Flowing with faith where hope abides.
Each droplet holds a sacred truth,
The promise borne from the fountain of youth.

Let us bend low, and drink this grace,
The essence of life we seek to embrace.
With eyes renewed, we see the way,
In every wave, a prayer to stay.

As evening falls, the shadows blend,
Grace's allure will never end.
In waters pure, we find our source,
A journey forward, a divine course.

## The Spiritual Odyssey

Upon the path, where spirits soar,
Each step a tale, an ancient lore.
In shadows deep, and valleys wide,
The heart ignites with the holy guide.

Mountains call with whispers bold,
In their silence, the stories unfold.
Through trials faced and bridges crossed,
The soul finds strength, never lost.

The stars above, like thoughts divine,
Each one a dream, a sacred sign.
In darkness found, the light will shine,
A journey vast, the heart's design.

With every breath, a prayer ascends,
To seek the truth, our journey bends.
In this odyssey, we rise and pray,
For every dawn brings a brighter day.

## **Pilgrimage to the Heart's Desire**

In lands afar, our spirits roam,
Each footfall leads us ever home.
Through valleys lush and barren plains,
The heart's desire in joy remains.

Across the fields where silence lies,
The echoes of faith reach for the skies.
In every heartbeat, every sigh,
A pilgrimage, where souls comply.

Through temples grand and humble shrines,
The essence of love in sacred signs.
With open hearts, we yearn to find,
The sacred thread that weaves mankind.

As we traverse this sacred quest,
In unity, our souls are blessed.
With open arms, the journey's art,
A pilgrimage to the heart's desire.

## Following the Footprints of the Ancients

In ancient lands where wisdom sleeps,
The footprints linger, the spirit leaps.
With every step, we trace the past,
In echoes vast, their shadows cast.

The elders whisper through the trees,
Their timeless tales upon the breeze.
Guiding us forth with gentle grace,
In every turn, we find our place.

With candle's light, we seek the truth,
In every moment, rebirth of youth.
With open hearts and eager eyes,
We honor those who've touched the skies.

As we walk on this chosen path,
In footsteps small, the sacred math.
Following light where spirits dwell,
A journey shared, a tale to tell.

## Quilted Memories of Divine Encounters

In whispers soft, the heavens speak,
Each moment stitched, a treasure unique.
With every tear, a blessing set,
In love's embrace, we shall not forget.

The stars align, a tapestry bright,
Guiding our hearts through the endless night.
Each memory a thread, woven with care,
In faith and hope, our souls laid bare.

Through trials faced, the spirit sings,
Echoing grace that each day brings.
In quietude, we find our way,
To heavenly realms where shadows sway.

In sacred circles, we gather near,
Embraced by love that casts out fear.
The quilt of life, rich and profound,
In Divine's hands, forever bound.

## **Under the Canopy of Grace**

In the garden where petals play,
We find solace in light's warm ray.
Each leaf a prayer, whispered soft,
Nurtured by faith, we rise aloft.

Beneath the boughs, a sacred trust,
In gentle rain, we find our must.
Shadows dance where sunlight streams,
Hope unfurls in vivid dreams.

When storms may come to test the night,
We cling to love, our guiding light.
In every drop, a lesson learned,
Through trials faced, our hearts will yearn.

United as one, our spirits soar,
Under grace's arch, forevermore.
In nature's hymn, we find our grace,
Enfolded warmly in its embrace.

## The Threshold of the Infinite

At the door where time does bend,
A realm awaits, where souls transcend.
Each heartbeat echoes a sacred name,
In the stillness, we fan the flame.

Glimmers of truth, like stars above,
Illuminate the paths of love.
Crossing over, we feel the call,
Embracing oneness through the all.

In silent prayer, the veils unfold,
Unlocking wisdom, deep and bold.
With open hearts, we pierce the veil,
In the embrace of love, we prevail.

In the ocean of light, we find our place,
Lost in wonder, wrapped in grace.
The infinite beckons, beyond the night,
Guiding us home to the source of light.

## The Dance of the Soul in Light

In the sacred rhythm, our spirits twirl,
A dance of joy, as blessings unfurl.
Each step we take is a prayer in flight,
Embracing love in the warmth of light.

With every breath, the universe sings,
Resonating through all living things.
In perfect harmony, we find our place,
The dance of souls, a divine embrace.

In stillness, we circle, hearts entwined,
Glancing within, the wondrous divine.
A movement soft like a gentle breeze,
Whispers of truth bring the heart to ease.

Together we glide through the cosmic sea,
Boundless and free, in unity.
In the dance of souls, we rise and soar,
Finding our home forevermore.

## Threads of the Divine Tapestry

In the loom of creation's might,
Threads of wisdom shine so bright.
Each strand a story, woven strong,
Echoes of love in every song.

From the hand that guides our fate,
Each knot reveals a sacred state.
Colors blend in a holy dance,
Inviting us to seek, to chance.

In every twist, a name is known,
Patterns that lead us back home.
With the fabric of faith entwined,
We find our purpose, divinely aligned.

So let us cherish this design,
Threads of the divine, intertwined.
Together woven, together spun,
In this tapestry, we are one.

## The Sacred Invitation

In the stillness of the night,
A whisper calls, soft and light.
An invitation to the soul,
To come and seek, to be made whole.

Underneath the ancient trees,
Spirit dances in the breeze.
Every rustle, every sigh,
A gentle beckon from on high.

To kneel in silence, hearts laid bare,
Breath of the sacred fills the air.
In every shadow, every beam,
The divine stirs, a humble dream.

So heed the call, let go of strife,
Embrace the journey, embrace the life.
In faith, we gather, in love, we soar,
To the sacred invitation that opens the door.

## Shadows of Grace Beneath the Stars

In the gaze of the twinkling night,
Shadows whisper, soft with light.
Graced by beams that spill like gold,
Stories of wonder waiting to be told.

Each constellation, a map of hope,
Guiding hearts as they learn to cope.
In the stillness, echoing praise,
We find our way through the darkened maze.

With arms outstretched to the skies above,
We seek solace, we seek love.
In the beauty of the quiet grace,
We find our truth in this sacred space.

So let us wander, let us expect,
Under the stars, we reflect.
In shadows of grace, our spirits dance,
A celestial chorus, a hallowed trance.

## Breath of the Cosmos

In the stillness where time stands still,
Breath of the cosmos, a sacred thrill.
Each heartbeat echoes vast and wide,
Life's rhythm flows like the ocean tide.

From the mountains tall to valleys deep,
Nature sings, awaken from sleep.
In every creature, a truth discerned,
The flame of creation, ever burned.

As we draw from this cosmic air,
In gratitude, we live, we share.
Breath by breath, our souls ignite,
In the dance of existence, pure and bright.

So let us honor this precious gift,
With every sigh, our spirits lift.
United in the breath of the divine,
In the cosmos' embrace, our hearts align.

## The Sacred Echo in the Wilderness

In the stillness of the night,
Whispers of the ancients bloom,
Leaves dance under lunar light,
Echoes break the solemn gloom.

Mountains high and rivers deep,
Nature sings of truths divine,
In her arms, my spirit leaps,
Beneath her gaze, the stars align.

Every step a prayer unfolds,
Every breath a hymn of grace,
In the wild where life beholds,
I discover love's embrace.

Here, the heart finds peace anew,
In the sacred, I will dwell,
Nature's voice calls soft and true,
In the wilderness, all is well.

## Clarity Beyond the Veil

Veils of shadows drift away,
In the light, my soul takes flight,
Truth illuminates the gray,
Guiding hearts towards the right.

Eyes once clouded, now awake,
Wisdom dances in the breeze,
Every choice, a path to take,
In the stillness, I find peace.

Voices echo from above,
Cleansing streams of holy thought,
Wrapped in grace, I feel His love,
In the quiet, truth is sought.

Beyond the veil, I shall tread,
With each step, a promise made,
In this journey, fears I shed,
In clarity, I am remade.

## Harmonics of the High Realms

Celestial choirs sing above,
Resonating through the night,
In their notes, the sound of love,
Shaping dreams, igniting light.

Every chord a sacred bond,
In this symphony of grace,
Heaven calls, my heart responds,
Lost in time and space, I trace.

Stars align to guide the way,
In their glow, I find my song,
Harmonies of night and day,
In this journey, I belong.

Music flows like rivers wide,
Singing praises, pure and true,
In the light, I will abide,
Harmonics of the high realms renew.

## In Search of Grace's Embrace

Through the valleys, I will roam,
Seeking where the whispers dwell,
In the silence, I find home,
Within my heart, I hear the bell.

Every step a search for light,
In the shadows, grace appears,
Hope and faith, my guiding sight,
Wiping away all the fears.

From the heavens, blessings pour,
Softly touching weary souls,
In her arms, I find the core,
As the spirit gently rolls.

In this journey, love's embrace,
Marks the path where I shall tread,
Finding solace in her grace,
In her warmth, my heart is fed.

## Whispers from the Eternal

In the silence of the night, we hear,
Soft murmurs of a love sincere.
Every heartbeat echoes true,
A sacred bond, me and you.

Stars above in heavenly grace,
Illuminate the timeless space.
In prayer's light, we find our way,
Guided by the dawn of day.

In shadows cast by doubt and fear,
Divine whispers are always near.
A calm embrace through trials faced,
In every tear, His love is traced.

Through valleys deep, we seek the light,
With faith our armor, shining bright.
In every step, His path we tread,
With whispers soft, our souls are fed.

## The Veil of Transcendence

Beyond the veil where angels sing,
Eternal truths their voices bring.
In realms where time cannot confine,
The spirit dances, pure, divine.

In moments brief, the heart takes flight,
Embracing love, the endless light.
With open arms, we journey far,
Guided by our shining star.

Through trials faced, our souls will rise,
Embracing hope beneath vast skies.
In whispered vows, we find our fate,
In grace, we learn to love, create.

In every breath, we sense the call,
The sacred bond that ties us all.
Through sacrifice and gentle grace,
We glimpse the truth in love's embrace.

## **A Pilgrim's Ascent**

With weary feet, the pilgrim walks,
Through winding paths where silence talks.
Each step a prayer, a quiet plea,
In search of truth, the soul set free.

The mountains rise, like faith untold,
Each peak a promise, pure as gold.
Through storms and trials, we ascend,
In every struggle, hope will mend.

Beneath the sky, our spirits soar,
In unity, we seek much more.
With open hearts, we share our grace,
In every bond, a sacred space.

In every dawn, new light appears,
As pilgrims shed their doubts and fears.
Through love's embrace, we find our way,
A journey blessed with each new day.

## Echoes of the Infinite

In the stillness, echoes call,
Whispers of love, embracing all.
In every heartbeat, grace defined,
Eternity within the mind.

Through time's embrace, we weave our song,
In sacred rhythms, we belong.
The fabric of our souls entwined,
In every loss, a truth aligned.

With every tear, a lesson learned,
The fires of faith, forever burned.
In unity, we stand as one,
Our hearts ablaze 'neath moon and sun.

In echoes vast, we find our peace,
A promise made, a sweet release.
In the infinite, our spirits bind,
In love's embrace, the truth we find.

## Whispered Prayers in Silent Woods

In quiet sighs beneath the trees,
The spirit's voice drifts on the breeze.
Each leaf a heart, a prayer they weave,
In secret glades, we believe.

Beneath the boughs, our hopes take flight,
Eclipsed within the soft moonlight.
They rise like smoke to heavens high,
In sacred silence, we reply.

The whispers share our deepest dreams,
In twilight's glow, where shadows gleam.
Each moment held, a treasure found,
In woodland peace, our souls are crowned.

Here in this realm, divinity shines,
In every breath, where love aligns.
We walk in faith, the path is clear,
With whispered prayers, God's voice we hear.

## The Ladder of Ascension

Step by step, we reach for grace,
With humble hearts, we seek His face.
Each rung we climb, a lesson learned,
In faith's embrace, our spirits yearned.

Through trials faced and burdens borne,
The spirit strengthened, hope reborn.
As clouds part ways, the light shines through,
In every climb, we find what's true.

The heights we scale, a glimpse divine,
With every prayer, our souls align.
Together bound, we rise above,
Our hearts ignited by His love.

On each ascension, grace descends,
A bridge to heaven, where love transcends.
In unity, we find our song,
The ladder leads, where we belong.

## Embracing the Celestial Tapestry

In threads of light, our stories gleam,
Woven dreams within His scheme.
With colors bright, our lives entwined,
In every stitch, His love we find.

The cosmos calls with every breath,
In sacred patterns, life and death.
We walk the fabric, hand in hand,
United souls with faith we stand.

Through trials faced, we learn to see,
The beauty in our tapestry.
Each moment shared, a sacred thread,
In every heart, His truth is spread.

Embrace the weave, let spirits soar,
In harmony, we seek the door.
To realms beyond, where love reigns free,
In the celestial tapestry.

## Wings of the Spirit's Ascent

With wings of grace, the spirit flies,
Beyond the clouds, to endless skies.
In holy whispers, we arise,
Transcending fears, to where love lies.

In every trial, we find our wings,
Embracing hope, the joy it brings.
Each beat a prayer, pure and bright,
In unity, we chase the light.

On zephyr winds, our dreams take flight,
Sustained by faith, we soar in might.
Together strong, our voices blend,
In spirit's dance, our hearts ascend.

In love's embrace, we're never lone,
With wings of faith, we've found our home.
To Him we rise, on high we sing,
In unity, our spirits wing.

## Visions of the Transcendent Flame

In the stillness of prayer, I see,
A flame that dances, wild and free.
Illuminating shadows deep within,
A whisper of light where silence begins.

Heavenly embers ignite my heart,
Filling the void, a sacred art.
Each flicker speaks of love untold,
In the warmth of the fire, I feel consoled.

The flame consumes all doubt and fear,
Drawing me closer, the path is clear.
With every heartbeat, I am renewed,
In the sacred warmth, my soul is brewed.

Transcendent flame, my guiding light,
In your embrace, darkness turns bright.
Through trials faced, I rise again,
With visions of hope that never wane.

## In the Presence of the Unseen

In quiet moments, I feel the sway,
Of presence guiding along my way.
Veiled in mystery, yet close at hand,
The unseen love in which I stand.

Whispers echo through the gentle night,
A touch of grace that feels so right.
Through the veil where shadows play,
I find the truth that won't decay.

With each breath, a heartbeat near,
The unseen dance, a melody clear.
In stillness deep, wisdom unfolds,
A story of love, eternally told.

In the unseen, I take my flight,
Wings of spirit, soaring in light.
Together we wander, heart and soul,
In the presence divine, I feel whole.

# Glimmers of Grace on the Horizon

Beyond the dark, the dawn does break,
Glimmers of grace in every wake.
Soft hues of hope touch the skies,
Illuminating hearts that rise.

Each day begins with promise anew,
A gentle kiss from skies so blue.
As light spills forth on paths we tread,
Faith ignites where shadows are shed.

In fleeting moments, I catch the light,
A spark of the sacred, pure and bright.
Through trials faced, I find my way,
As grace unfolds at the break of day.

On the horizon, love does gleam,
A beacon of light, a holy dream.
With every step, I walk the line,
Glimmers of grace, forever divine.

## The Divine Odyssey Within

Within the heart, a journey starts,
A quest for truth that never departs.
Through valleys deep and mountains high,
The divine odyssey, spirit's cry.

Each step I take in sacred ground,
Unraveling mysteries I have found.
In the depths of silence, I hear the call,
The echo of love that binds us all.

Waves of insight rise and fall,
Revealing wisdom in every thrall.
The path may twist, the road may bend,
But the journey within has no end.

Through storms and trials, I persevere,
With every heartbeat, I draw near.
The light within guides my way,
On this divine odyssey, come what may.

## In Search of the Divine Echo

In quiet whispers, spirits call,
In the stillness, we hear it all.
Heaven's beams light the darkened way,
Guiding seekers to hope's bright ray.

Through valleys low and mountains high,
We lift our hearts to the endless sky.
In every prayer, a soft refrain,
The echo of love, beyond all pain.

With every step, the path unfolds,
In truth and grace, the heart beholds.
A journey woven with sacred threads,
In the divine embrace, our spirit treads.

In search of light, we rise and sing,
To the sacred source, our souls take wing.
Through trials faced and burdens shared,
The echo of faith shows we are cared.

## Crossing the Threshold of Eternity

Upon the shore of endless grace,
We stand before the timeless place.
With every breath, we sense the call,
To leave behind the earthly thrall.

Hands entwined, we step beyond,
Into the light, our hearts respond.
In silence deep, the truth is found,
As spirit dances, woven round.

The threshold whispers ancient lore,
Of lives lived vast, and love's rapport.
We cast away our worldly chains,
In eternity, our spirit reigns.

With open hearts, we move as one,
To cross the line where all is done.
In the embrace of the sacred night,
We find our way, in purest light.

## **Navigating the Waters of Faith**

In the depths of the soul's wide sea,
We seek the beacon, wild and free.
The currents may crash and winds may cry,
But hope's bright sail will soar the sky.

With every wave, lessons unfold,
In prayers whispered, stories told.
Through trials harsh, and calm's sweet embrace,
Faith's compass guides us, finds our place.

The waters churn, we set our course,
Through faith's rich tapestry, we draw force.
The stars above, our map of grace,
In navigating darkness, we see His face.

Together we journey, hand in hand,
In the liquid depths of faith's grand strand.
With love's fierce tide, we rise and glide,
In harmony with the divine inside.

## Lanterns for the Soul's Voyage

In the night where shadows creep,
We hold our lanterns, light to keep.
Each flame a prayer, a gentle spark,
Guiding us through the cold and dark.

As we traverse the winding road,
With faith ablaze, we share our load.
These lanterns shine, a sacred art,
Illuminating the weary heart.

We gather strength from each small light,
In unity, we conquer night.
With every flicker, we find our way,
In the darkest hours, hope will stay.

So let us walk, the path adorned,
With lanterns bright, our souls reborn.
In the circle of light, love's embrace,
Together we sail, in light's vast space.

Milton Keynes UK
Ingram Content Group UK Ltd.
UKHW022124291124
451915UK00010B/510

9 789916 878545